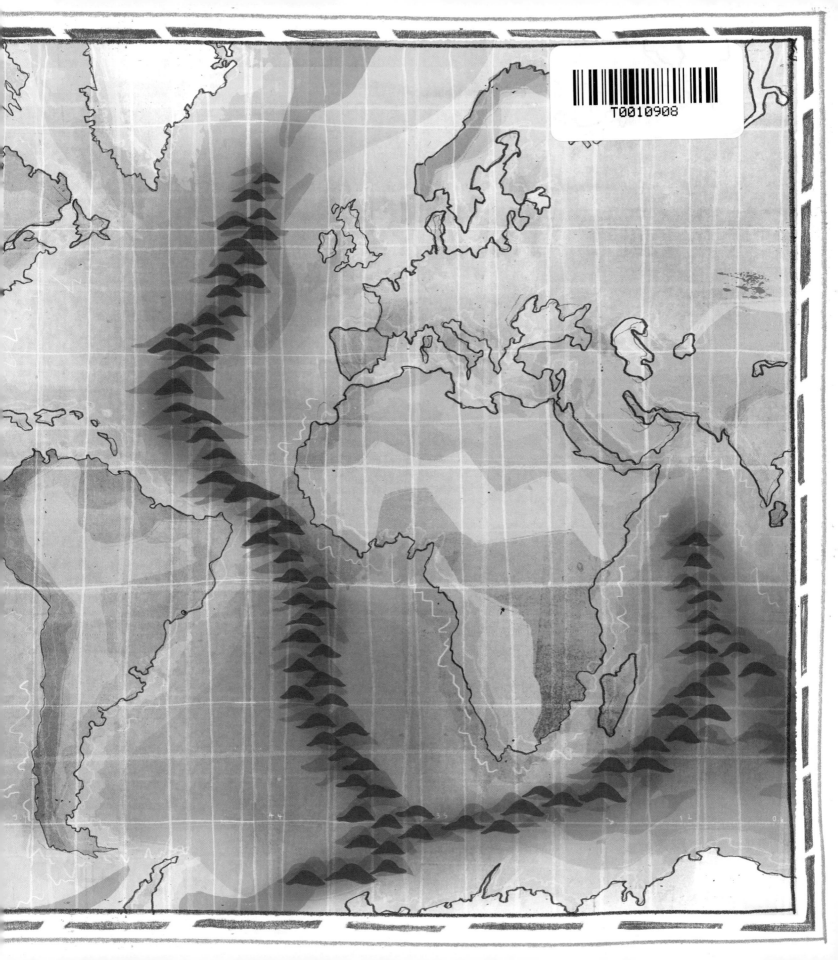

OCEAN SPEAKS

HOW
MARIE THARP
REVEALED
THE OCEAN'S
BIGGEST
SECRET

WORDS BY
Jess Keating

PICTURES BY
Katie Hickey

tundra

The beach was a blanket of squishy, soft sand, and Marie wanted to feel it under her feet.
Shoes off.
Socks off.
The ocean stretched out before her, like a big blue mystery.

The waves were talking to her, whooshing up
to her toes and sighing away again.

Marie loved going into the countryside with her father to search for treasures. She discovered forests and farmhouses, boulders and birdcalls, wheat fields and waterfalls. Marie's curiosity was as big as the world she wanted to explore.

ANGLERFISH

When she was old enough, Marie wanted to study the earth like her Papa. She wanted to be surrounded by rocks and trees, soil and mountains, sunlight and fresh air.

But those were jobs for boys, not girls. When Marie was growing up, girls were not supposed to dream of becoming scientists or explorers.

Instead, she had to take art classes.

Marie sketched in her notebook. She learned about stylish outfits, shapes and designs. And she stuck her sculptures together with gum.

Marie did not take art for long.

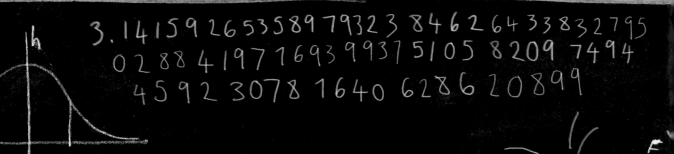

$$3.14159\,26535\,89793\,23\,846\,2\,64\,3383\,2795$$
$$0288\,4197\,1693\,9937\,5105\,8209\,7494$$
$$4592\,3078\,1640\,6286\,20899$$

Soon, many men went off to fight in a war. With the men away, women were encouraged to learn science. Marie saw her chance. She began studying geology, math, chemistry and physics. There was so much to explore! She discovered geodes and geometry, equations and elements, atoms and antimatter.

$$a^2 + b^2 = c^2$$

$$6\,CO_2 + 6\,H_2O \longrightarrow C_6H_{12}O_6 + 6\,O_2$$

$$\left(\frac{\partial U}{\partial T}\right)_V = T\left(\frac{\partial S}{\partial T}\right)_V\left(\frac{\partial U}{\partial S}\right)$$

$$\frac{-b - \sqrt{(b^2 - 4ac)}}{2a}$$

$$\frac{-b + \sqrt{(b^2 - 4ac)}}{2a}$$

$$x = \frac{-b}{2a}$$

$$y = ax^2 + bx + c$$

$$\left(\frac{-b}{2a}\middle|\frac{1 - (b^2 - 4ac)}{4a}\right)$$

$$y = -1 - (b^2 - 4ac) \over 4a$$

$$\left(\frac{-b}{2a}\middle|\frac{-b^2 - 4ac}{4a}\right)$$

physica ARISTOTLE

Under a Lucky Star CHAPMAN ANDREAS

One, Two, Three... GAMOW

Marie was so proud when she got her first job in a laboratory in New York. When her male colleagues returned from the war, they were sent on research trips. Marie wished she could go too.

They were sailing the Atlantic Ocean, using high-frequency sounds to explore the ocean floor. They got to work with the sun on their skin and salt in their hair.

But women were considered bad luck on ships. Marie wasn't allowed to join her colleagues. She had to stay behind.

Box after box full of depth measurements were sent back to the office. Marie's job was to use the data to create a map of the ocean floor, plotting every point on paper.

She knew the ocean and its secrets were inside these boxes. So she set to work.

Marie's fingertips became stained with ink. Eraser shavings fell to the floor. Her drafting lamp hummed beside her.

She had found another way to follow her dream. With her map, she could be an explorer after all.

Instead of the vast, open ocean,
she dove into her tiny, cramped office.

Instead of crashing waves,
she sailed through reams of smooth paper.

$$e^{i\pi} + 1 = 0$$
$$e^{iu} = \cos(u) + i\sin(u)$$
$$\Delta d_x = (v_x)t$$
$$\Delta d_y = (v_{iy})t - \frac{1}{2}gt^2$$

$$1 = 0.99999999999999999\ldots$$

Instead of clouds,
she dreamed of calculations.

And instead of the dark,
mysterious ocean depths,
she swam through bottles of
pitch-black ink.

Marie mapped point, after point, after point.
Inside her small office, Marie's map grew bigger.

6.6

5.3

5.01

3.9

2.1

1.96

And bigger.

And bigger.

Soon, Marie wasn't in her office anymore. She was an explorer on the ocean floor, surrounded by valleys and peaks, mountains and canyons, dips and hills.

After weeks of work, Marie looked at her map. Something was wrong. There was a deep rift valley on the floor of the Atlantic Ocean. A long crack, with mountainous peaks on both sides.

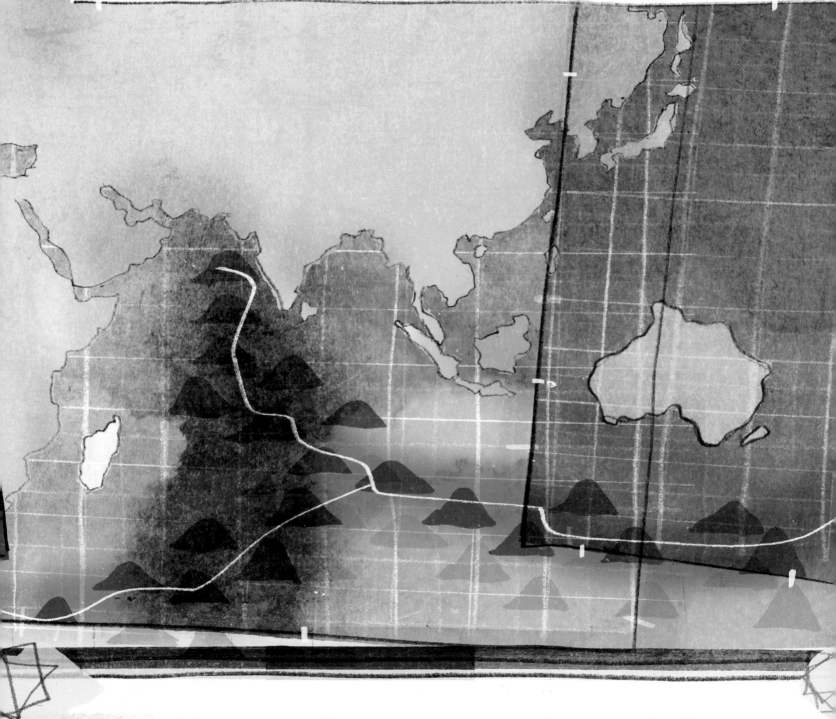

The ocean was talking to Marie again. But what was it telling her?

Marie showed the map to her colleague. He yelled. He argued. It must be a mistake, nothing but foolish, silly girl-talk. He told Marie to redo her work. She knew her map was correct and was eager to prove it.

Marie dove into her paper ocean once more. And again, the great rift valley appeared. Like a seam on a baseball, the rift circled the Earth on the ocean floor. Earth's crust appeared to have moved and shifted apart somehow.

Despite her evidence, nobody believed in Marie's work. One man, an explorer named Jacques Cousteau, decided to prove her wrong. He sent his cameras down, down, down.

He expected to film an empty ocean floor with no rift valley in sight.

He was wrong.

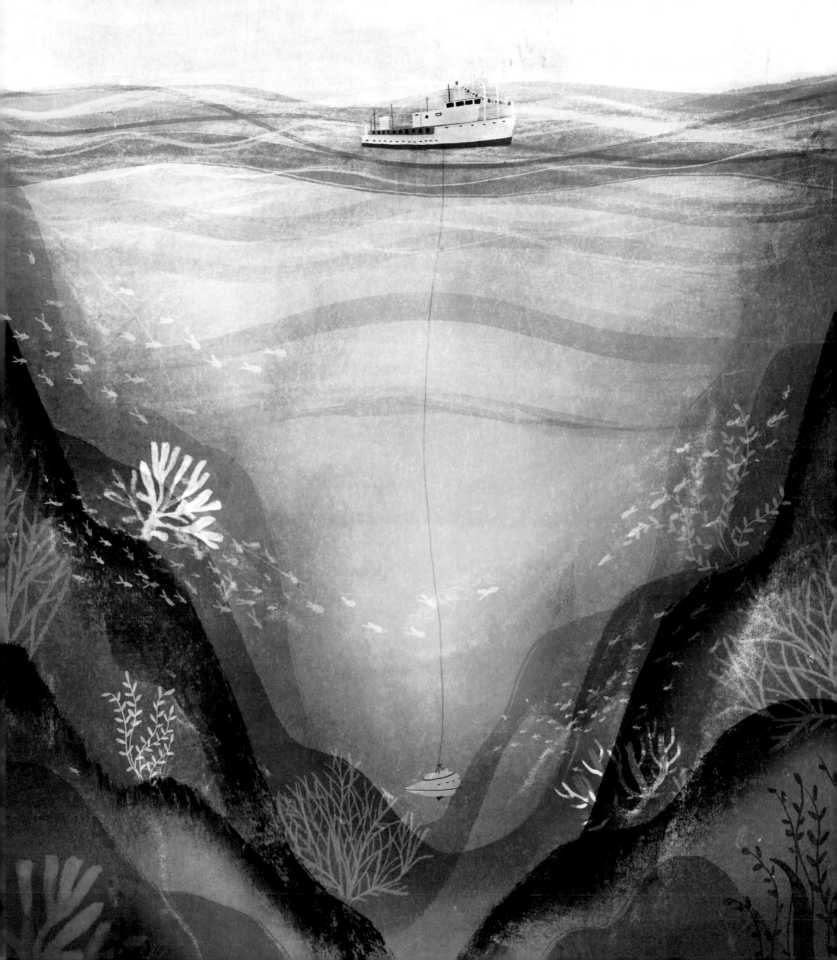

Marie's map had revealed the ocean's biggest secret. The rift valley was as real as any valley on land. There were mountains beneath the waves, hidden by the ocean's great depths. Marie had discovered what would soon become the largest known mountain range on our planet.

Her map became famous. Because of it, scientists started wondering. How did the ocean floor move like this? Was it still moving? What other truths could we learn by studying the hidden depths? Marie's map opened the door for us to better understand our planet.

The next time Marie visited the ocean, she listened
to it whoosh and sigh around her.

She felt the sun on her skin and the salt in her
hair. And she smiled.

Author's Note

Marie Tharp (1920–2006) was an American geologist and oceanographic cartographer, which is a fancy way of saying she knew a lot about rocks and earth science, and even more about the bottom of the ocean. Marie's map not only *depicted* a huge rift in the world, it *caused* one. To understand why, we need to become explorers ourselves and dive into history.

Around 300 million years ago, Earth didn't have the seven continents that exist today. Instead, it had one big supercontinent, which we now refer to as Pangaea. So how did we end up with seven continents? Today, scientists believe that all continents rest on enormous slabs of rock. These slabs are always moving, interacting with each other and shifting over time. This process is known as plate tectonics.

But before Marie's time, the concept of plate tectonics wasn't known. Some scientists had believed that the continents had once been close together, but it was difficult to explain how they had moved. In 1912, Alfred Wegener was the first scientist to propose that the continents were once a giant land mass that drifted apart. This theory was known as continental drift, and while he had some evidence of the movement of continents, he couldn't explain *how* the movement happened. Ultimately, he was attacked viciously and mocked for this theory, and any mention of continental drift became extremely taboo in the scientific world.

It was still taboo when Marie and her map came along in 1957. Because her map looked like it supported the idea of continental drift, Marie was told to redo it. She did, and the rift appeared again. It looked like the earth had moved and split apart, leaving behind a huge scar with mountains on each side. Furthermore, Marie and her colleagues learned that the rift and mountains they had mapped were part of a larger system of underwater mountain ranges, spanning 40,000 miles (65,000 kilometers) and wrapping around Earth like the seams of a baseball. (Note that the image in this book of the baseball with seams depicts all of the major underwater mountain ridges;

however, at the time in the story, Marie had only mapped the mid-Atlantic ridge.)

Marie had mapped the truth. She believed in her work and stood tall as others doubted it. Her colleague and friend Bruce Heezen presented the map on her behalf. It took several years for other scientists to embrace Marie's map, but once they did, people began to once more examine how the continents might move over time. From there, the discovery of tectonic plates was only a step away.

The continents are still moving today, but Marie's map remains fixed as a crucial yet overlooked key to our understanding of earth science. In 1997, Marie's map was displayed in the Library of Congress, alongside the journals of Lewis and Clark and the original draft of the Declaration of Independence. She was also named one of the four greatest cartographers of the twentieth century.

Throughout her life, Marie worked in the background. But, like the shifting earth she mapped so beautifully, Marie proved that those in the background can have incredibly powerful influences on the world. Her legacy lives on in all those who explore the big blue mystery of the ocean realm.

Questions and Answers

What is sonar, and how can we map the ocean floor with it?

Sonar is a way of measuring distance that uses sound. With a device called a transducer, a sound wave is sent into the water. The pulse of sound then travels to the bottom of the ocean, where it bounces off the ocean floor. The bouncing sound wave reflects back, and is picked up by the transducer. By measuring how long the sound takes to bounce back in different areas, scientists are able to build an image of the peaks and valleys of the ocean floor. Sound waves return very fast in shallow water and slower in deeper water.

Why weren't women welcome in the sciences when Marie was studying?

When her map was first presented, Marie was not credited, and it wasn't until years later that she became known for her brilliant work. This is because throughout history, women have not been treated equally in many ways. Sometimes, certain jobs were only given to men, because it was assumed they were stronger or smarter. This couldn't be further from the truth! Today, women still face prejudices in their fields of work, and women around the world are fighting for equal rights.

Can I see the mid-ocean ridge?

The mid-ocean ridge is the largest mountain range on Earth, but most of it is located more than 1.2 miles (2000 meters) underwater. It is possible to see a small section of it in Iceland, where the ridge rises above sea level. This part of the ridge is called Reykjanes Ridge and is a segment of the larger mid-Atlantic ridge.

What is geology? How can I become a geologist?

Geology is the study of solid earth and the processes that form it. This includes rocks, metals, oils and other resources. We can learn a lot about Earth's history by studying these materials, and geologists may specialize in several fields. Volcanology (the study of volcanoes), paleontology (the study of fossils) and pedology (the study of soil) are all branches of geology.

In order to become a geologist, you can start by reading and exploring! Your librarian or teacher can help you find books about rocks, Earth's history and land formations, and you can even keep a notebook yourself of all your discoveries as you explore your own community.

Further Reading

Brake, Mark. *The Big Earth Book*. Oakland, CA: Lonely Planet Global, 2017.

Felt, Hali. *Soundings: The Remarkable Woman Who Mapped the Ocean Floor*. New York: Henry Holt, 2012.

Romaine, Garret. *Geology Lab for Kids: 52 Projects to Explore Rocks, Gems, Geodes, Crystals, Fossils, and Other Wonders of the Earth's Surface*. Beverly, MA: Quarry, 2017.

Tharp, Marie. "Connect the Dots: Mapping the Seafloor and Discovering the Mid-Ocean Ridge." In *Lamont-Doherty Earth Observatory: Twelve Perspectives on the First Fifty Years, 1949–1999*, edited by Laurence Lippsett. Palisades, NY: Lamont-Doherty Earth Observatory of Columbia University, 1999.

For a detailed look at Marie Tharp's map, visit the Library of Congress: https://www.loc.gov/resource/g9096c.ct003148/

To all the explorers with curious minds and adventurous hearts, I can't wait to see how you move the Earth — J.K.

For my Grandad Alan, thank you for showing me the shannies, limpets and the teeny tiny queenie shells — K.H.

Tundra Books, an imprint of Tundra Book Group, a division of Penguin Random House of Canada Limited

Library and Archives Canada Cataloguing in Publication

Title: Ocean speaks : How Marie Tharp revealed the ocean's biggest secret / Jess Keating, Katie Hickey.
Names: Keating, Jess, author. | Hickey, Katie, illustrator.
Identifiers: Canadiana (print) 20190091797 | Canadiana (ebook) 20190091835 | ISBN 9780735265080 (hardcover) | ISBN 9780735265097 (EPUB)
Subjects: LCSH: Tharp, Marie—Juvenile literature. | LCSH: Cartographers—United States—Biography—Juvenile literature. | LCSH: Women cartographers—United States—Biography—Juvenile literature. | LCSH: Geomorphologists—United States—Biography—Juvenile literature. | LCSH: Submarine topography—Juvenile literature.
Classification: LCC GA407.T43 K43 2020 | DDC j526.092—dc23

Published simultaneously in the United States of America by Tundra Books of Northern New York, an imprint of Tundra Book Group, a division of Penguin Random House of Canada Limited

Library of Congress Control Number: 2019938103

Photograph of Marie Tharp courtesy Lamont-Doherty Earth Observatory and the estate of Marie Tharp.

Edited by Elizabeth Kribs
Designed by John Martz
The artwork in this book was created with watercolor, pencil and mono-printing, and assembled digitally.
The text was set in Centaur MT Pro.

Printed in India

www.penguinrandomhouse.ca

2 3 4 5 6   26 25 24 23 22

tundra | Penguin Random House
TUNDRA BOOKS